SWEET
RUIN

The Brittingham Prize in Poetry

The University of Wisconsin Press Poetry Series
Ronald Wallace, General Editor

Places/Everyone • Jim Daniels
C. K. Williams, Judge, 1985

Talking to Strangers • Patricia Dobler
Maxine Kumin, Judge, 1986

Saving the Young Men of Vienna • David Kirby
Mona Van Duyn, Judge, 1987

Pocket Sundial • Lisa Zeidner
Charles Wright, Judge, 1988

Slow Joy • Stefanie Marlis
Gerald Stern, Judge, 1989

Level Green • Judith Vollmer
Mary Oliver, Judge, 1990

Salt • Renée Ashley
Donald Finkel, Judge, 1991

Sweet Ruin • Tony Hoagland
Donald Justice, Judge, 1992

SWEET
RUIN

Tony Hoagland

The University of Wisconsin Press

The University of Wisconsin Press
1930 Monroe Street, 3rd floor
Madison, Wisconsin 53711-2059
uwpress.wisc.edu

3 Henrietta Street
London WC2E 8LU, England
eurospanbookstore.com

Printed in the United States of America

Library of Congress Cataloging-in-Publication Data
Hoagland, Tony
Sweet Ruin / Tony Hoagland
92 pp.   cm. — (The Brittingham prize in poetry)
ISBN 0-299-13580-2   ISBN 0-299-13584-5 (pbk.)
I.   Title.   II. Series.
PS3558.03355S93   1992
811'.54—dc20   92-50252

ISBN-13: 978-0-299-13584-3 (pbk.: alk. paper)

For my brother Chris,
my brothers David Rivard and Dean Young,
and Betty Sasaki

C O N T E N T S

CONTENTS

Part 4

ACKNOWLEDGMENTS

Grateful acknowledgment to the publications where some of these poems first appeared: *American Poetry Review, Chiaroscuro, Cimarron Review, Crazy Horse, Denver Quarterly, Georgia Review, Mazagine, Passages North, Ploughshares, Poetry, Shankpainter, Sonora Review, Intro 13, Telescope,* and *Indiana Review.*

"One Season" appeared in the anthology *The Best of Crazy Horse,* University of Arkansas Press, 1990.
"Sweet Ruin" appeared in *The Pushcart Anthology: Best of the Small Presses,* Pushcart Press, 1991.
"Poem For Men Only," "One Season," and "Sweet Ruin" appeared in the anthology *New American Poets of the 90s,* published by Godine Press, 1991.

Special thanks to David Rivard, Steve Orlen, Tess Gallagher, Rolly Kent, and Gibb Windahl for their help with this manuscript. Thanks to the Provincetown Fine Arts Work Center, the Arizona Commission on the Arts, and the National Endowment for the Arts for their fellowships and grants. Residencies at Yaddo and the Centrum Foundation were also helpful in completing this book. To Carl Dennis, for his inspiration and support, great thanks.

I'd further like to thank my earlier publishers, Michael Bowden of San Pedro Press, David Duer of Coffeehouse Press, and Nard Taiz of Moon Pony Press. And certain others for their valuable friendship: Jane Chatterson Miller, David Schweidel, Mary Clark, John Fortier, Suze Stone, Rolf Jordahl, Bill W., Van Morrison, Barbara Cully, and Dean Young. My gratitude to you.

Part 1

My Destination

I gave orders for my horse to be brought round from the stable. The servant did not understand me. I myself went to the stable, saddled my horse and mounted. In the distance I heard a bugle call, I asked him what this meant. He knew nothing and had heard nothing. At the gate he stopped me, asking: "Where are you riding to, master?" "I don't know," I said, "only away from here, away from here. Always away from here, only by doing so can I reach my destination." "And so you know your destination?" he asked. "Yes," I answered, "didn't I say so? Away-From-Here, that is my destination." "You have no provisions with you," he said. "I need none," I said, "the journey is so long that I must die of hunger if I don't get anything on the way. No provisions can save me. For it is, fortunately, a truly immense journey."

—Franz Kafka

Perpetual Motion

In a little while I'll be drifting up an on-ramp,
sipping coffee from a styrofoam container,
checking my gas gauge with one eye
and twisting the dial of the radio
with the fingers of my third hand,
looking for a station I can steer to Saturn on.

It seems I have the travelling disease
again, an outbreak of that virus
celebrated by the cracked lips
of a thousand blues musicians—song
about a rooster and a traintrack,
a sunrise and a jug of cherry cherry wine.

It's the kind of perceptual confusion
that makes your loved ones into strangers,
that makes a highway look like a woman
with air conditioned arms. With a
bottomless cup of coffee for a mouth
and jewelry shaped like pay phone booths
dripping from her ears.

In a little while the radio will
almost have me convinced
that I am doing something romantic,
something to do with "freedom" and "becoming"
instead of fright and flight into
an anonymity so deep

it has no bottom,
only signs to tell you what direction
you are falling in: CHEYENNE, SEATTLE,
WICHITA, DETROIT—Do you hear me,

do you feel me moving through?
With my foot upon the gas,
between the future and the past,
I am here—
here where the desire to vanish
is stronger than the desire to appear.

Poem for Men Only

It wasn't easy, inventing the wheel,
dragging the first stones into place,
convincing them to be the first house.
Maybe that's why our fathers,
when they finished work,

had so little to say. Instead,
they drifted—feet crossed on the divan,
hands folded over stomachs like a prayer
to middle age. They watched the game,
or snored and dreamed of flying naked

through a storm of bills. When,
like a weighty oak, my father fell,
chopped down by a streak
of lightning through his chest,
when he went on living at the height

of an adjustable bed,
below a chart of pulse and respiration lines,
then I understood what it meant to be a man,
and land on your back in the shadow

of all your solitary strength,
listening to the masculine tickertape of leaves
whisper judgmentally above you.
Weakness is so frightening. You speak
from the side of a sagging mouth,

hear a voice you never wanted to produce
ask for some small, despicable, important

thing—a flexible straw, a crummy channel
change. I stared through the window,
across the institutional lawn,

seeking what to feel. Sparrows
darted to and from a single
emerald pine, a sort of bird motel.
Light purred into the grass. I tried
to see all men as brief

as birds—inhaling the powerful oxygen,
flying the lazy light, having their afternoon
as sort of millionaires,
then at evening, to reenter the collective shade
and shrink, remembering their size. When I looked

for my father, when my father finally
looked for me, it was impossible. We kept
our dignity. But when did I learn
to leave everyone behind? When did I get
as strong as my old man? Out of your strength,
you make a distance. Then you see,

and start to cross. You think
of what you want to say,
and you forget, deliberately.
Go back to the beginning. Think about it.
Take, if you like, all day.

Oh Mercy

Only the billionth person
to glance up at the moon tonight
which looks bald, high-browed and professorial
   to me,

the kind of face I always shook my fist at
when I was seventeen
and every stopsign was a figure of authority

that had it in for me
and every bottle of cold beer
had a little picture of my father on the label

for smashing down in parking lots
at 2 AM, when things devolved
into the dance of who was craziest.

That year, if we could have reached the moon,
if we could have shoplifted the paint and
   telescoping ladders,
we would have scribbled FUCK YOU

on its massive yellow cheek,
thrilled about the opportunity
to offend three billion people

in a single night.
But the moon stayed out of reach,
imperturbable, polite.

It kept on varnishing the seas,
overseeing the development of grapes in Italy,
putting the midwest to bed

in white pajamas.
It's seen my kind
a million times before

upon this parapet of loneliness and fear
and how we come around in time
to lifting up our heads,

looking for the kindness
that would make revenge unnecessary.

My Country

When I think of what I know about America,
I think of kissing my best friend's wife
in the parking lot of the zoo one afternoon,

just over the wall from the lion's cage.
One minute making small talk, the next
my face was moving down to meet her

wet and open, upturned mouth. It was a kind of
    patriotic act,
pledging our allegiance to the pleasure
and not the consequence, crossing over the border

of what we were supposed to do,
burning our bridges and making our bed
to an orchestra of screaming birds

and the smell of elephant manure. Over her shoulder
I could see the sun, burning palely in the winter sky
and I thought of my friend, who always tries

to see the good in situations—how an innocence
like that shouldn't be betrayed.
Then she took my lower lip between her teeth,

I slipped my hand inside her shirt and felt
my principles blinking out behind me
like streetlights in a town where I had never

lived, to which I never intended to return.
And who was left to speak of what had happened?
And who would ever be brave, or lonely,

or free enough to ask?

One Season

That was the summer my best friend
called me a faggot on the telephone,
hung up, and vanished from the earth,

a normal occurence in this country
where we change our lives
with the swiftness and hysterical finality

of dividing cells. That month
the rain refused to fall,
and fire engines streaked back and forth crosstown

towards smoke-filled residential zones
where people stood around outside, drank beer
and watched their neighbors' houses burn.

It was a bad time to be affected
by nearly anything,
especially anything as dangerous

as loving a man, if you happened to be
a man yourself, ashamed and unable to explain
how your feelings could be torn apart

by something stoical and unacknowledged
as friendship between males.
Probably I talked too loud that year

and thought an extra minute
before I crossed my legs; probably
I chose a girl I didn't care about

and took her everywhere,
knowing I would dump her in the fall
as part of evening the score,

part of practicing the scorn
it was clear I was going to need
to get across this planet

of violent emotional addition
and subtraction. Looking back, I can see
that I came through

in the spastic, fugitive, half-alive manner
of accident survivors. Fuck anyone
who says I could have done it

differently. Though now I find myself
returning to the scene
as if the pain I fled

were the only place that I had left to go;
as if my love, whatever kind it was, or is,
were still trapped beneath the wreckage

of that year,
and I was one of those angry firemen
having to go back into the burning house;
climbing a ladder

through the heavy smoke and acrid smell
of my own feelings,
as if they were the only
goddamn thing worth living for.

The Delay

I should walk up the stairs right now
and make slow love to the woman I live with,
but I sit here drinking gingerale instead
and turning the pages of a book

about the polar expeditions—men
who ran away from what they should have done
to carve a name out for themselves
in a hunk of planetary ice.

In the yellowed, hundred-year-old photographs,
they still look arrogant and brash
in their brand new bearskin coats and beards.
They might be Nordic gods, posing on a ridge

above a caravan of Eskimoes and sleds.
But I wonder how they looked months later,
when the emptiness they wanted
such a close inspection of

had eaten out their cheeks, eaten up
the part of them made out of words,
and left the bony, silent men themselves,
walking over fields of sea-green,

thousand-year-old ice and wind. There are
other photographs—the Welshman
kneeling, as if to pray,
at the carcass of a seal; Peary

weeping at the stump of his left hand.
There are other plot-lines and motifs.
But the story stays the same: some of us

would rather die than change. We love
  what will destroy us

as a shortcut through this world
which would bend and break us slowly
into average flesh and blood.
I close the book and listen to the noises

of an ordinary night. A chair that scrapes.
The cricket, like a small appliance
singing. The air of every room
so ponderously still. I can tell

that it is not too late.
And then I think this ordinariness
will crush me in its fist.
And then I wish it would.

for Charlie Smith

Sweet Ruin

Maybe that is what he was after,
my father, when he arranged, ten years ago,
to be discovered in a mobile home
with a woman named Roxanne, an attractive,
recently divorced masseuse.

He sat there, he said later, in the middle
of a red, imitation-leather sofa,
with his shoes off and a whiskey in his hand,
filling up with a joyful kind of dread—
like a swamp, filling up with night,

—while my mother hammered on the trailer door
with a muddy, pried-up stone,
then smashed the headlights of his car,
drove home,
and locked herself inside.

He paid the piper, was how he put it,
because he wanted to live,
and at the time knew no other way
than to behave like some blind and willful beast,
—to make a huge mistake, like a big leap

into space, as if following
a music that required dissonance
and a plunge into the dark.
That is what he tried to tell me,
the afternoon we talked,

as he reclined in his black chair,
divorced from the people in his story
by ten years and a heavy cloud of smoke.
Trying to explain how a man could come
to a place where he has nothing else to gain

unless he loses everything. So he
louses up his work, his love, his own heart.
He hails disaster like a cab. And years later,
when the storm has descended
and rubbed his face in the mud of himself,

he stands again and looks around,
strangely thankful just to be alive,
oddly jubilant—as if he had been granted
the answer to his riddle,
or as if the question

had been taken back. Perhaps
a wind is freshening the grass,
and he can see now, as for the first time,
the softness of the air between the blades. The pleasure
built into a single bending leaf.

Maybe then he calls it, in a low voice
and only to himself, *Sweet Ruin.*
And maybe only because I am his son,
I can hear just what he means. How
even at this moment, even when the world

seems so perfectly arranged, I feel
a force prepared to take it back.
Like a smudge on the horizon. Like a black spot
on the heart. How one day soon,
I might take this nervous paradise,

bone and muscle of this extraordinary life,
and with one deliberate gesture,
like a man stepping on a stick,
break it into halves. But less gracefully

than that. I think there must be something wrong
with me, or wrong with strength, that I would
break my happiness apart
simply for the pleasure of the sound.
The sound the pieces make. What is wrong

with peace? I couldn't say.
But, sweet ruin, I can hear you.
There is always the desire.
Always the cloud, suddenly present
and willing to oblige.

Proud

Like those crazy Babylonians, who raised a tower
higher than their own I.Q.; so gigantic,
it could only have been built by God—
a fact that they forgot, until they fell,
in argument, apart, like so many unmortared

parts of speech. Babylon, remember?
They fell, and we grew up
to learn two languages—one for money,
and one for love; one for saying what we mean,
and one for hiding it. I'm thinking of my brother,

who lost his voice, and then his wife
because he was too proud to say, "Please, Don't Go."
That architect, my brother,
who sleeps now on his office couch,
twitching like a racedog in a business suit,

a dog who dreams he is so far ahead of all
the competition, he'll be impossible to catch.
I'm speaking of my brother, but I might as well
be talking of my enormously rich and arrogant
other relative, the United States—a country so goliath,

it casts a shadow over half the world;
so ambidextrous, it can lie and listen to itself
at once. And isn't that the story of the mind?
Which started as a little church,
with open doors,

but wound up as a fortress, with foot-thick walls
and a bristling defense. Somewhere inside,

we are lost, muttering about our enemies
and making up the truth. Truth is,
the self is a disease, a wound

which grows infected with the fear
that it will never have enough.
And egomania
is standing on a mountaintop
and sucking down great lungfuls

of a better quality of air
than what the common people get; it feels
like freedom and it tastes like truth;
you laugh, and every forty seconds, pledge
a new allegiance to yourself. And maybe

we will have to go on climbing to some
hopeless height, to some fantastic speed,
like Icarus the biggest day of his career.
Maybe there are pinnacles of ignorance,
altitudes of stupid, from which

recovery is impossible. I think
of my brother, who might have saved himself
with just a single word, however late and lame.
I think of my country,
which goes on talking.

Part 2

"Nature is good because she is the daughter of God,"
　　Umbertino said.
"And God must be good, since he generated nature,"
　　William said with a smile.

—Umberto Eco, *The Name of the Rose*

Second Nature

I must be enjoying my sixth or seventh life by now,
watching the orange, early morning sun
gleam thickly through the fabric of an evergreen

as the smoke churns dark and sap-like up,
then wafts away from the chimneyspout.
In the past, when I heard people talk about

how a place becomes a part of you,
I always thought that they were being metaphorical,
but right now I can feel this orange and tender light

taking a position inside of me—
painting a stripe of phosphorescent,
pumpkin-colored warmth along one wall

of the inside of my skull. I can feel
the washed-out scarlet of these winter fields
becoming an ingredient

of my personality,
the way that in the noisy urban center
of every molecule of chlorophyll,

one atom of magnesium resides,
as quiet and essential as a church.
Seated in appreciation of this calm,

in the easy chair of my appreciation,
I have a view of what has brought me here—
not just the landscapes I've survived,

not just the blind motion of the waves,
but what I grasped and made a part of what I am—
a second nature, scavenged from those things

I chose to love or fear.
There was a sycamore in Arizona I cared
enough about to take into my heart, and now

I hear the wind moving through its branches
just below my clavicle. There was a kiss
that changed the history of my mouth—kiss

that was a courtship, marriage and divorce
sandwiched in the thirty-second intersection
of her lips and mine. When I look

at all the odds and ends I'm made of,
I think I'm just some kind of
irrationally-proportioned

Frankenstein,
on pilgrimage to god knows where,
humming a song as he lumbers through the forest

of the middle of his life.
His left eye still remembers
a sunset that it saw in 1964; his right

beholds the snow upon a branch
with so much childish love
it threatens continually to break

the rockpile of his heart.
But he keeps going on,
half-thrilled and half-appalled

by his own strangeness—wondering what god
he could be fashioned in the image of?
What handiwork of what mad scientist?

Carnal Knowledge

The night your girlfriend
first disappeared beneath the sheets
to take you in her red, wet mouth
with an amethystine sweetness

and a surprising expertise,
then came up for a kiss
as her reward,
you had to worry whether you could taste

the faint flavor of your own
penis on her soft peach lips,
and what that possibly could mean
was an idea so charged

it scorched the fragile circuits
of your eighteen-year-old
imagination,
though by now you were beginning to suspect

that everyone
lived a secret life of acts
they never advertised,
and you were right.

Maybe that was the evening
you began to learn
how to swallow
what you couldn't understand

in the name of love;
what it felt like to be entered
by something strange
for pleasure's sake.

And afterwards,
did you look into the distance of the dark
and smoke a cigarette
and feel a little foreign to yourself?

as someone does who has been changed
by a single unexpected drop of life?

The Question

"We are what is missing from the world."

—Fernando Pessoa

Some questions have no answer.
Raised, they hang there in the mind
like open mouths, full of something missing.
The great Portuguese poet, Pessoa,
said that the idea of happiness
is what makes men permanently sad.
The body, imagining the soul,
looks ugly to itself.
A man hears a word, and the world
becomes a place that he misunderstands.
So he climbs high into his life,
ashamed of all he doesn't know,
and refuses to come down.

If you could coax him out again,
you could tell him, say,
that anything can be explained.
The shape of apples, for example,
by their love of travel.
Or that the sky is blue because
it's an easy color on the eyes.

Even the dog, chasing its tail,
has, temporarily, a center.
Even the bird, disappearing into its hole
knows that the world goes on without it.
And Pessoa, that eminently healthy man,
that artist, wore a blue wool hat
even on the hottest summer days.

Simply to toss at strangers on the street.
He liked to see them catch it,
and grow immediately less strange.

A Dowry

You could say that they have talent,
those sheaves of flowers
embroidering the hill above the bay,
with their blues and saffrons,
their nipples and pajamas.
You could say that they have talent,
but no ambition,
just beauty and good luck,
living at the crossroads
of chlorophyll and light.
You could say what you like
as a way to keep from
giving in to them. They can wait.
Nothing puts them in a rush
but the gusts of ocean wind
for which they bend and straighten.

All morning on my five-mile hike,
I've crossed these provinces of color,
inventing crazy names and throwing them away
like paper airplanes
from a child's fat hand: *Chinaman's Trousers*,
Blue Horsehooves, the thorny
Mother-In Law's Revenge—naming them
to please myself, to pollinate
the stubborness of facts with words.

If you were here, this landscape
wouldn't stand a chance—
we'd walk all afternoon,
talking and complaining of our lives.
You'd make reference, straddling a fence,
to St. Paul's view of sin. I'd describe

the splash of auburn freckles
on my ex-lover's inner thigh. We'd have
a good time in our way.
And I both love and fear
our restless, half-pleasureable pride
in discontent. As if we thought that exile
were a manly art. As if heaven
were everything we're not.

So today I let myself be talked to
by one plum-colored weed,
dipping on its stalk—a swoon
so drunk and delicate,
it hurt.
And brother, isn't this the moment
for which we hoard our separateness?
Doesn't every Abner and Jean-Paul
have a price for his dissatisfaction?
—a dowry,
for which he would become
simple as a flower,
a modest blossom called *Sweet Idiot*,
or *Narcissist's Demise?*—a flower
without talent or ambition
—just beauty, which is the lifelong friend
of beauty, just
beauty and the light for friends.

for David Rivard

You're the Top

Of all the people that I've ever known
I think my grandmother Bernice
would be best qualified to be beside me now

driving north of Boston in a rented car
while Cole Porter warbles on the radio;
Only she would be trivial and un-

politically correct enough to totally enjoy
the rhyming of *Mahatma Ghandi*
with *Napoleon brandy*;

and she would understand, from 1948,
the miracle that once was cellophane,
which Porter rhymes with *night in Spain*.

She loved that image of the high gay life
where people dressed by servants
turned every night into the Ritz:

dancing through a shower of just
uncorked champagne
into the shelter of a dry martini.

When she was 70 and I was young
I hated how a life of privilege
had kept her ignorance intact

about the world beneath her pretty feet,
how she believed that people with good manners
naturally had yachts, knew how to waltz

and dribbled French into their sentences
like salad dressing. My liberal adolescent rage
was like a righteous fist back then

that wouldn't let me rest,
but I've come far enough from who I was
to see her as she saw herself:

a tipsy debutante in 1938,
kicking off a party with her shoes;
launching the lipstick-red high heel
            from her elegant big toe

into the orbit of a chandelier
suspended in a lyric by Cole Porter,
bright and beautiful and useless.

Two Shades of Orange

It must be something like a bouquet for Him,
   Our Lord, watching from great height,
      when the garbagemen bang shoulders
with the flock of Hare Krishnas
   at the cross roads of Ashby and Van Ness
—the orange and saffron uniforms
   of the flowers in His garden
      issuing forth, blossoming:
pan handlers and can handlers,
   barefoot and booted,
      skullshorn and unshaven,
      And see—a traffic signal standing in
for Moses and his rod—how the tide
   of early morning traffic parts
      to allow safe passage of the tribe
from one curb to the next.
      He catalogues
each callous on each foot, the empty eye
   of each missed bootlace hole, each daub
      of trash compactor-generated primal
mire, smeared upon the jumpsuit monogram.
      He knows Vishnu, Johnson and
Rodriguez, knows
   their addresses and wives'
      favorite technicolor lipstick-flavored
         kiss-techniques.
How great His appetite!
   How marvelous the scope of His buffet,
      the raucous welter of particulars
He loves—more ever than we can,
   who are the agents of His presence,
as we maneuver through His premises,
   and complicate His pleasure

when we avert our eyes
from one another's souls,
as the very hungry will.

Doing This

I'm driving back and forth
on the gravel lane
before the two-room, stucco house

of the woman I love. She's inside,
making love with a woman
whose white car is parked in the driveway

and it, this car, disturbs me
more than anything. It sticks out of itself
so far into my life. Each time I pass,

I know, with a ten-pound sadness in my chest,
that I can't keep doing this.
And now I realize, far too late,

I should have fought for her, should have
wept and begged and made the full,
hair-extracting spectacle

of what I felt. I should have
shed my pride.
What good is pride? When you die,

I know they turn you
inside out, to see what portion
of your god-allotted guts

you failed to spend on earth.
The ones who arrive in heaven
without a kopek of their fortune left

are welcomed, cheered, embraced.
The rest are chastised and reborn
as salesmen and librarians.

It's so simple,
and that's what gets me—that every time
I drive up and down this street,

looking at that white Toyota in the drive,
it messes up not just this life,
but my eternity as well.

But I keep doing it,
dragging myself back and forth
over this corner of the world

which scrapes and grinds against me,
like a rock on the bow of a ship.
Etching the errors in my surface

deeper, and deeper. And less forgiven.

The Word

Down near the bottom
of the crossed-out list
of things you have to do today,

between "green thread"
and "broccoli," you find
that you have pencilled "sunlight."

Resting on the page, the word
is beautiful. It touches you
as if you had a friend

and sunlight were a present
he had sent from someplace distant
as this morning—to cheer you up,

and to remind you that,
among your duties, pleasure
is a thing

that also needs accomplishing.
Do you remember?
that time and light are kinds

of love, and love
is no less practical
than a coffee grinder

or a safe spare tire?
Tomorrow you may be utterly
without a clue,

but today you get a telegram
from the heart in exile,
proclaiming that the kingdom

still exists,
the king and queen alive,
still speaking to their children,

—to any one among them
who can find the time
to sit out in the sun and listen.

Volunteer

This is not the moment
to be rounded off
by a turn-of-the-century
childhood memory,
or the expiration
of a favorite aunt; not
the occasion to elucidate
a painting by Degas.

I'm not suggesting that we pass a law
against the past,
or try to close the factory
responsible for making sense,
—only that it might be nice
to wallow in the present for awhile,
it might be practical

to occupy the molecules
in the very nether surface
of your fingertips
at the instant they make contact
with a cold doorbell
or a warm girl. Do you
agree?

    All the time we've saved
since we stopped praying for our souls
hasn't filled the hole
inside the human gut; hasn't
stopped the human nervous system
from being very nervous.
                But maybe,

if we listen hard
we can find the frequency,
the still point in the center of the wave
where history stops repeating its instructions,
and leaves some room to breathe.

It is a simple task—
just the job, on any given day,
of raising the whole world
above your head—
one aspirin, one teacup,
one traffic ticket at a time;

the way a volunteer might raise his hand
to apply for evolution,
even though it means
the possible extinction
of his former personality,

even though it means replacing
what is right in front of you
with what is right in front of you
again and again
with a vigorous insistence
until the moment and the room
are one.

Oh lord,
allow me to continue
to preach your gospel
of rock and roll
among the deaf and dear defeated
creatures of the heart.

Shield us from the fear
which translates as fatigue;
retrain our minds from their unhappiness,
and make our lives the theatre
for many strange delights

for which we'll twist and shout,
and sometimes even sing,
as if we didn't know the meaning
of the word *responsibility*,
or as if part of our responsibility
belonged to joy.

Part 3

"I" at the wrong time brings a curse.
"I" at the right time gives a blessing.
If a rooster crows early, when it's still dark,
he must have his head cut off.

—Rumi

In the Land of Lotus Eaters

What was the name of that bronze-headed stud
of a Greek deity
in charge of the Temple of Distraction?
Around whose shrine the ancient Greeks
would congregate, like flies, for hours,
instead of working in their shops and fields?

I remember dying for a drink
about the time my grandmother was ready
to say her final words into someone's ear.
I remember seeing, in the air above her head,
among the tubes and stainless steel,
a vision of a speedboat

with a laughing girl on board,
a red speedboat with the word
ALOHA stencilled on the bow,
ready to take me anywhere.
I guess I'm just the kind of person

who needs to be continually reminded
about love and brevity, about diligence
and loyalty to pain. And maybe my attention
is just permanently damaged, never coming back
from too much television,
too much silly talk,

the way Ulysses' men turned into swine
from too much recreation in the Lotus Land,
then ran away because they couldn't
stand to see what they'd become.

That's why the newsreels of Cambodia must be divided
   into slices
by deodorant commercials,
why the lipstick shades to choose between in
   drugstores
equal the number of remaining whales.
That's why the demolition of the rain forest
is directly proportionate to the number of couples
entering therapy in Kansas City.

It is as if, in another version of the *Odyssey*,
Ulysses' men forgot to tie him to the mast,
and he abandoned ship
to chase the luscious acapella voices of the sexy siren
   sisters.
To chase and chase and chase and chase and chase and
   chase.

And the archers shot their arrows with their eyes
   closed.
And the workers in the factory denied any knowledge
of what the weapons would be used for.
And the name of the one in charge was forgotten.
And the boat sailed on without a captain.

The Collaboration

That was the summer I used *The Duino Elegies*
in all of my seductions,
taking Rilke from my briefcase

the way another man might break out
candlelight and wine.
I think Rilke would have understood,

would have thought the means
justified the end, as I began to read
in a voice so low it forced my audience

to lean a little closer,
as if Rilke were a limestone bench
stationed on a hillside

where lovers gathered to enjoy the vista
of each other listening.
What a chaperone,

and what a view—is it Susan
I am thinking of?—
how, in the middle of the great *Ninth Elegy*,

in the passage where the poet
promises to memorize the earth,
her tanned and naked knee

seemed the perfect landing platform
for any angels in the vicinity.
I think Rilke would have seen

the outline of an angel
in the space between our bodies
just before we kissed,

then seen it vanish
as we clashed together
and commenced our collaboration

on another chapter
of the famous, familiar and amusing
saga of human relations—choosing

heat instead of grace,
possession over possibility—trading
the kingdom of heaven

one more time
for two arms full
of beautiful, confusing earth.

History of Desire

When you're seventeen, and drunk
on the husky, late-night flavor
of your first girlfriend's voice
along the wires of the telephone

what else to do but steal
your father's El Dorado from the drive,
and cruise out to the park on Driscoll Hill?
Then climb the county water tower

and aerosol her name in spraycan orange
a hundred feet above the town?
Because only the letters of that word,
DORIS, next door to yours,

in yard-high, iridescent script,
are amplified enough to tell the world
who's playing lead guitar
in the rock band of your blood.

You don't consider for a moment
the shock in store for you in 10 A.D.,
a decade after Doris, when,
out for a drive on your visit home,

you take the Smallville Road, look up
and see *RON LOVES DORIS*
still scorched upon the reservoir.
This is how history catches up—

by holding still until you
bump into yourself.

What makes you blush, and shove
the pedal of the Mustang

almost through the floor
as if you wanted to spray gravel
across the features of the past,
or accelerate into oblivion?

Are you so out of love that you
can't move fast enough away?
But if desire is acceleration,
experience is circular as any

Indianapolis. We keep coming back
to what we are—each time older,
more freaked out, or less afraid.
And you are older now.

You should stop today.
In the name of Doris, stop.

Properly

Look at this woman, properly
a little gawky
to compensate for
being beautiful,
—how her pale breasts dangle
in a sky blue shirt
arched above her cat.
Who is this character
in the sunlit living room
and how did she become so
willing to embrace you
at the fateful juncture
of a telephone directory
and a tropical plant?
Doesn't she remind you
of a sunset or a drug
to make you talk? You think
Columbus may have felt like this,
sailing closer to the shore
that turned him into an American.

You have travelled far
as in a fairy tale
and passed through many arms
like foreign lands,
but now you are rather
like a child, just trying
to stand still—a man
who would believe in anything
credible enough to get
his mouth mixed up with hers.
The first kiss must be
very softly launched,

not to change the shape
or subject of these lips
into those of others you have
known—like footsteps which,
having got you here,
now need to be forgotten
so that history might
lie down and be made.

Men and Women

I don't understand why this woman
crushes ice into a glass, adds
honey, mint, and strong dark tea,

then brings the glass to me;
or why she sings, self-consciously
when she believes I'm watching

the bowcurve of her sunburned collarbone
as she moves between the bedroom
and the bath. And I can't

imagine what she thinks
is worth staying around for
after we've made love or eaten dinner,

after we've taken our walk
a long ways in one direction
and talked ourselves so thoroughly

inside out,
no urgency for speech remains.
Birds settle in the trees,

and this pale, sinking,
salmon-colored light
lingers inordinately

all over the horizon,
while I get a great desire
to quit while I'm ahead,

take the car from the garage and go
zoom, zoom, around the bend
before I shatter everything

from nervousness that anything
can last. If things are given time,
they take on weight.

They are commissioned.
Without a word, one day
they will require loyalty.

Travellers

In the coffee shops and restaurants,
the airport terminals and lounges,
the lovers are debating
the pleasures of presence versus
the pleasures of absence,

drawing diagrams and dotted lines
in the wet glassrings left behind
by other customers,
building little barricades and highways
out of breakfast crumbs.

And if, looking up, they find that they've arrived
at no conclusions,
who can blame them?
—considering the mileage on certain parts
of the vocabulary,

considering they've been stranded
once or twice before
upon the road between desire
and its destination—like a car
that's out of gas,

or a noun without an adjective.
Still they want so much
to mash their faces
into the mushy sky of something warm
and human; want to make some sweeping declarations
about the rest of their existence;
want to flap their arms

and swear that they can fly.
No jury would convict them
of anything but being hungry
for proof of their existence,

anything but the bigamy of marrying
their favorite mistake
one time or two too many.

So he draws a line of water on formica,
like a car following a highway
between A and C. She rubs a circle
in a splash of tea
like the circle you might clear

in the breath-fogged window of a speeding train.
He shreds a napkin into triangle-shaped bits;
she pierces them with toothpicks,
and together they have fashioned
the small white flags of their surrender,

the truce with fear
that lets them move a little farther out
into the foreign country
of the future
where all of us are strangers.

Geography

For the last few seconds now
I have been travelling

up one slope and down the other side
of some of those unchristianed hills

we could call your breath.
Hello. Tonight I have only

my impossibility to thank
for letting me propose

that landscapes know when they are loved.
That light, when it approaches earth,

slows down
to take on passengers

without misshaping them.
That's right. This coastline flies.

En route between the ends and means
it demonstrates affection

by bending towards the harbor
of a nightingale

or dreaming up the grenadine effect
of dawn on a guitar. Oh my.

Why did we bother to invent a god
when every common thing

elicits and supports a miracle,
issues light like a command?

I could love you, probably,
with more perspective

from the narrow, straight-backed chair
in the adjoining room—or,

granted that hypothesis,
from a chalet on the moon.

But then I wouldn't get to trace
the steep, unfolding curves

of your geography;
then I wouldn't get to watch

the wave your eyelashes will make
as they rise

and the whole world
moves away from you.

A Love of Learning

He knows it is absurd,
he should not care
for all of Yugoslavia
because her hand happens,
for a moment, to reside

on that bluegreen corner
of the classroom globe;
and that it is ridiculous
for streaks of chalkdust upon a dress
to assume the resonance

of brushstrokes by Renoir,
But that is how love goes,
leaping like a goat
from point to point,
without a thought of falling

through the holes in scholarly
responsibility.
The course is called AFFECTION
BY ASSOCIATION,
and anyone enrolled soon learns

that love spreads out, proliferates,
infects—not unlike
the spread of gunpowder
from east to west, or Christianity

in the opposite direction—until
what started with one person
carrying a torch

illuminates a landscape
with the fever of a sensibility.

Out the lunchroom window now,
he sees the willow trees
are rooted in devotion,
and every slender branch
provides the wind a chance

to get acquainted with a plant. And
isn't that what we desire?
An endless introduction
to a subject with no end?

Isn't that what we require?
Always to believe
that we are practicing a word
which will survive
the worst pronunciation?

—to *become* that word,
and feel surrounded by
the constant stirring
of love's immense vocabulary—
like the rustling of wind

through the grove of earthly things—
as it composes
phrases, sentences and signs.

Paradise

When my dear zooms off
In her smart grey tweed,
All shoulderpads and scimitar lapels
For a thoroughly executive evening
At the office,

The kiss she leaves imprinted on my lips
Glows with exactly the smudged glow
Of the smouldering peach clouds
Above the bay.

        It's a late-model
Sunset, slung low
On the corporate skyline
In a turn-of-the-century city
Thriving on illusions—see how they wink

& advertise themselves—
A million thrills
Rising in thin air,
A million rooms at the top
Of the carpeted stairs,
Where the high-boned priests and priestesses work late

While the night, expresso-black, encamps
Upon the town
And all the neighbors blink, and arm themselves
With frequencies and charms
To carry off all thinking,
All dark forebodings
That pleasure forbids.

Part 4

And the more you do it
the more that it becomes
a beautiful obsession.

—Van Morrison

Tom-tom, c'est moi.

—Wallace Stevens

Ducks

A pair of fat, iridescent ducks
struggling to lift
from the green-grey surface of a lake
upon the dentist's office wall
reminds you of the anywhere you'd rather be

as he keeps bringing you back
into the world of gravity
and shrill, bone-corroding drills,
making you pay for all those years
you wasted thinking about

things less real than tooth decay.
In the thin, fluorescent light the ducks
look like an endangered species,
with their heavy, satin bellies
slung low above the pointy waves—

but still, their plumage glows,
and you can see that this is the essential
confrontation—pain and beauty
braced against each other
like a pair of teeth,

a tug of war
in which the prize is you
and whether you will swallow or spit out
this contradictory life.

So you relax, lean back, and open wide,
letting science pave the inside of your mouth
with painkillers and gold.
But you keep looking at the ducks—

long necks outthrust, intent
on their ascent
towards some distant patch of sky
which won't exist
until they get to it.

Like you, they have a motive,
they have an opportunity.

                              for Jack Myers

All Along the Watchtower

I remember the pink, candy-colored lights
strung around an auditorium
shaped like an enormous ear
and a single, distant figure on a stage, gripping a guitar
that twisted like a serpent

trying to turn into a bird.
Sixteen, high on acid for the first time,
I flew above the crowd in a cross-legged position,
down corridors embroidered with my
dazzled neural matter. And all those arms,
adrift like wheatstalks in a storm, reached up
to touch the flank of something bright, and warm.

Talking 'bout my generation,
that got our instructions for living
from the lyrics of rock and roll
then blasted off into the future
with our eardrums full of scar tissue
and a ridiculous belief in good vibrations.

God of micrograms and decibels,
shirtless deity of drum solos and dance,
you fooled us good
over and over,

and we found out, again and again,
you couldn't hold a bolt of lightning
very long
you couldn't spend a lifetime
on the spire of a moment's exultation.

But the lit-up sign that says *Now Playing*
on the back wall of the brain
still leads me down
to that small illuminated stage,

and I swear that he's still standing there,
the skinny figure in a tank top and old jeans—
a glittering guitar raised in his right hand
like a beacon on a psychedelic tower—,
I can hear the thunder and the reverb

while the band plays on,
I can taste the drugs and candy-colored light—
and the adolescent hunger for *more life more life more life*
still flashing, still calling out
like a warning, and a summons.

Emigration

Try being sick for a year,
then having that year turn into two,
until the memory of your health is like an island
going out of sight behind you

and you sail on in twilight,
with the sound of waves.
It's not a dream. You pass
through waiting rooms and clinics

until the very sky seems pharmaceutical,
and the faces of the doctors are your stars
whose smile or frown
means to hurry and get well

or die.
And because illness feels like punishment,
an enormous effort to be good
comes out of you—
like the good behavior of a child

desperate to appease
the invisible parents of this world.
And when that fails,
there is an orb of anger

rising like the sun above
the mind afraid of death,
and then a lake of grief, staining everything below,
and then a holding action of neurotic vigilance

and then a recitation of the history
of second chances.

And the illusions keep on coming,
and fading out, and coming on again

while your skin turns yellow from the medicine,
your ankles swell like dough above your shoes,
and you stop wanting to make love
because there is no love in you,

only a desire to be done.
But you're not done.
Your bags are packed
and you are travelling.

Threshold

When I see the thick blue cable of a vein
running through a woman's bony hands

beside me in the supermarket checkout line,
I look sideways to make sure

that her back is slightly hunched,
that her hair is thin and lusterless

and that she holds a wallet so engorged
with chargecards and ID

it has the bulk and contour of a battered heart;
I check the way the bones poke, clotheshanger-like,

through the thin shoulders of her dress
and how the swollen-knuckled fingers shake

when they attempt to clasp the buckle of her purse,
so that the customers in line behind her

shift their feet and sigh,
then roll their eyes

as a coin slips out of her grasp—
I make certain her complexion

has the moist, chalky, spotted pallor
of long illness, or long reclusiveness,

and that the skull is pushing outward
through the mask of skin and hair

like a rock bulging in the surface of a stream,
and if all these signs are visible,

then I know that it is you,
and I am standing in the presence of the stain

of death on life,
and I hold still and inhale deeply

as if mortality
were a kind of fancy French perfume.

Safeway

Even after an hour in her room
with eyeshadow and rouge,
moisture whip, lip gloss, and perfume
my mother still looked like she was dying

unexotically,
still looked like a person
trying to impersonate a person
going somewhere other than the grave,

though she was only going to the store,
after weeks of living
horizontally
while her blood was scoured by detergents
bleached by blasts of subatomic light.

Riding on her bony little head,
the glossy auburn wig
looked like something stolen,
the lame hip pulled her to one side
like the stuck wheel of the shopping cart we pushed

past pyramids of fruit,
down mile long corridors of breakfast food
where cartoon animals shot sugar stars
over an infinity of bowls,

—a landscape which seemed,
in the brightness and abundance of its goods,
like somebody's idea
of paradise—

and the bright, continual ringing of the registers
was like the sound of happiness
for sale.

I was angry, dutiful, and seventeen,
afraid she was going to read her obituary
in the faces of the shoppers;

frightened they would stop and stare
at the black cloud hovering above our heads
as we moved slow as history
up and down the aisles.

Maybe months of sickness had burned away my
        mother's shame
and left in her dry mouth
a taste for irony, maybe she wanted
to show the populace

what death looked like in person
or maybe it was simply her last chance
to make small talk with the neighbors
who stopped to say hello—

Mrs. Johnson, Mrs. Green,
whose kindness I imagined, then despised,
caught awkwardly among them as I was,
between the living and the dead.

But looking back across the years,
the scene looks different to me now. I see
a little group of people, halted
in the midst of life,
their carts jammed up
against the lettuce and the tangerines.

There is no gallows standing there,
no spectral executioner fingering his blade.

And I seem sweet at seventeen, innocent
even in my rage—
trying to protect
what didn't need protecting
from what couldn't be saved.

Smoke

God, it is good to wake
    in the middle of the night
        and smoke a cigarette
with You,
        while outside, the buildings sleep
            in geometric clumps,
the factories rest—replenishing
        themselves, not so unlike
            the rosebushes or
eucalyptus groves,
        gathering power
            for one more thrust tomorrow.
For now,
        the streetlights blossom
            above the boulevard,
a lone truck on the darkened bridge
        transports its spark across the gap,
            the way your fingertip
ignited Michaelangelo to think,
        long ago,
            that You were there.
One does so much
        building up, so much feverish
            acquiring,
but really, it is all aimed
        at a condition of exhausted
            simplicity, isn't it?
We don't love things.

So this hour of the night
    is precious,
        when the curtains swell like lungs

and the world is full of bodies
    falling from the precipice
        of sleep.
For seven hours,
    maybe eight, they don't
        remember how to suffer
or how to run from it.
    They are like the stars,
        or potted plants, or salty oceanic waves.
And do You like this brand of cigarette?
    And are You comfortable?
        It is so quiet now,
the streetlights shine.
    And I have noticed
        how the strands of smoke,
even in no hint of wind,
    still decorate the air
        in cursive braided loops and swirls.
No, it is not a signature.
    But it is beautiful,
        and it is inexplicable,
and it is good.

Astrology

It's so clear tonight, and calm,
that if I stepped outside,
and raised my head, I imagine
I could see the silver

chest hairs of Orion,
the hummingbird tattoo upon
the outside of his thigh.
And further back, the unfathomable

dark, which makes it possible for him
to draw his bow,
and gives him room to choose
a target for the night.

So I remember the luxury of what
I've had the poor taste in the past
to call, sometimes, our loneliness,
which is the absence of others

who have left us stranded here,
with only oxygen to breathe
and nothing more than time
to breathe it in.

And I honor, for a moment, the million
things forgotten, the things
which have so graciously
forgotten me—the bulging

saddlebags of history, the myriad, self-cancelling
blunders and eurekas

of fathers and mothers
of fathers and mothers and fathers—

who have handed down something
of tremendous importance
by handing down nothing
but plenty of quiet and dark.

And in the fields of sky above our houses,
these well-lit
hieroglyphics, open to
our own interpretation.

In Gratitude for Talk

The blue-grey steeples of the pines,
the lake's cold oval:
is there anything to which
we won't assign a shape?
Like tourists living on the shore
of what really matters,
we can lean back in our chairs and say,
"Those clouds are marble quarries,"
or, "Life would be much simpler
if people were like birds."
And sometimes, between the thick brushstrokes
of what we plan to see,
we glimpse the thing itself:
the water sliding under its description.

Our broad disagreement
on the nature of god
must make him very happy
when he returns, late at night
to eavesdrop from the dark just off the porch—
to us, tossing marked cards
at an imaginary hat
and telling stories to stay warm:
how the sparrows got into the stars
and ate them up like breadcrumbs,
or about the man who was so perverse
he ended each relationship
just when it was perfect.

If there's no future in the dark,
I think that it increases
the value of just sitting here,

getting drunk on talk. You can't
ignore the dark for god's sake,
or argue against faith.
The porch swing creaks that old tune,
"Maybe, Maybe Not,"
and discussions end like this—
each voice pushing off into the silence,
like men in boats;
as if they were certain of their fates,
or had chosen their indifference.
But now the silence has a different shape.

A Change in Plans

It's tiring, this endless revision
of our idea of a world
which is being continually revised—
as the painter good-naturedly lengthens
the ash on his model's cigarette—or,
if nature is his model, subtracts a leaf
from the birch undressing in the yard.

It's hard to remember
what we're practicing for
with this long succession of goodbyes
as each new understanding
goes out of date, like a window
turning into a mistake.

What we've learned is mostly
not to be so smart—to believe,
as the hands believe,
in only what they hold.
And we don't rush our explanations.
Instead, we tell a story:

Remember how the reptiles,
after generations of desire
to taste the yellow flowers,
thrust out wings one day and lifted from
    the ground?
Being birds by that time,
their appetites had changed.
But they kept on flying.